Seeing
and
Proclaiming
Alaska's
Destiny

Seeing and Proclaiming Alaska's Destiny

*Compiled, Scribed and Prayers
by Deborah A. Rubey*

XULON PRESS

Xulon Press
2301 Lucien Way #415
Maitland, FL 32751
407.339.4217
www.xulonpress.com

Printed in the United States of America.

ISBN-13: 978-1-6312-9202-6

Foreword

G od is continually speaking for those who have an ear to hear. Psalm 19 says that the heavens are declaring the Glory of God. The day pours out His speech and the night reveals His knowledge. In her book " Seeing and Proclaiming Alaska's Destiny", Deb Rubey has collected much of what God has said about Alaska.

This is very important because God has spoken prophetically over every state, but not every state has a collection of these prophetic words. What Deb has done in this book provides not only a written record of what God has said, but a valuable tool for intercessors who watch over the words and prophets who declare the words and worshipers who sing the words and many others who, in various ways, will release these words of the Lord into the atmosphere and the land of the state of Alaska.

Isaiah 55:5-11 says that the word of the Lord will accomplish what it is released to do. Jeremiah 1:12 says that the Lord watches over His word to perform it. His word must first be released before He can watch over it and cause it to accomplish what He sends it to do. This book will facilitate the release of the word of the Lord for Alaska so that He can watch over it and cause it to accomplish His purposes.

Not only has Deb complied these words, but she has provided a faith response in the form of prayers based on these words. While not everyone will pray the prayers exactly as written, they provide a starting point for responding to the words God has released. For those who are new to praying in response to the prophetic word, these prayers will help you to increase your faith response to prophetic words.

When God releases prophetic words, He watches to see what we do with them and how we respond to them. If we are faithful with little, more will be given. As the intercessors, prophets, pastors and church in Alaska begin to respond to these words, we can expect to watch and see them fulfilled. We can expect for more words to be given and we can expect to see Alaska become who God has called her to be, according to His word.

I believe that individuals, intercessory groups, churches and the State of Alaska will all benefit from this book. Thank you, Deb, for your time and effort in bringing this gift to us.

Linda Heidler
Glory of Zion Ministries

Yes, I want to lift up my Jesus, He is the reason. The reason I was born is to worship Him. For He captured my heart with His love and I have never been the same. My beautiful Jesus.

I would like to mention, with honor, my mother, Margorie Halpin. Who moved to heaven in 1992 at the young age of 54. She was a prayer warrior before anyone talked about warring in prayer. She prayed for her children daily, and heard from the Lord what was in His heart for each one of us. I know that her prayers she prayed, moved heaven on my behalf. For I cried out to the Father, He pulled me out of the miry pit and set my feet upon the Rock of Jesus.

I want to encourage all who have prodigal children, don't stop praying, don't stop warring, don't stop decreeing and declaring the Word of the Lord over them. Trust …. And believe… and Love them. Love them, for God hears the cry of those prayers and petitions, and the bowls are filling up. They are being poured out…upon those loved ones.

To all those that have spoken into my life over the years, with Kingdom wisdom.

I say, how can I thank you? For this book is a fruit of some of those words you spoke to me and over me. I pray this fruit have seed and produce more fruit.

I would like to thank a dear friend, Debra Marsh, for the hours of assisting me in spelling, punctuation and editing in the processing of getting this book ready for the publisher.

What a treasure you are to me. Thank you, my God given friend.

I would like to honor Mary Glazier, as the keeper of the prophetic words for Alaska from 1986 into the early years of the 2000's. Thank you Mary for your faithfulness in preserving the writings of these words. The fruit of your labor is now and will be evident for generations.

There are so many that I have known and so very many I have never known that have poured into this Great Land and the people of Alaska.

There are not a few that have served on kingdom assignment, and poured into this state with their heart and soul, causing a shift that has changed the atmosphere and changed generations yet to come.

All those who served, ministered and gave of their lives on behalf of Alaska, it is because of your saying "Yes", to the Lord, that Alaska is moving forward into this new season.

Those ministries that are opening doors for the Body of Christ, thank you.

Each one is so important in the whole of Alaska.

Each one has an assignment and part in the coming together of this state.

You know who you are, you have prayed for His fire to spread throughout this state, causing unity and one accord amongst the Bride in Alaska.

Your faith has sparked courage with the fruit of mighty warriors for the Lord.

Thank you is not enough; your reward is in heaven.

Endorsements

"As I read these words of prophesy, I am reminded of II Chronicles 20:20 "believe in the Lord your God and you shall be established, believe His prophets and you shall prosper".

It's clear that our acceptance has to do with our personal prosperity and welfare. However, we must also consider 1 Corinthians 14:29 "let two or three prophets speak and let the others judge". This means the word spoken, must not conflict with scripture or otherwise misdirection.

I have confidence in Deborah Rubey's judgement of their validity and am pleased she would take the time and effort to compile this valuable information for us. Too often we only hear a prophesy and are not able to assimilate the fullness of the message. I encourage readers to give careful attention to these words of prophecy. God does talk to us through His prophets. Give them due consideration and pray for their fulfillment."

Dick Strutz

Dick is a lifelong Alaskan, his family having lived in Anchorage, Alaska for over 100 years.
He was saved in 1953 and started in full time ministry in 1972 when he founded the Charismatic Bible College, at Abbott Loop Community Church. This played a major part in starting over 50 new churches throughout the United States. Dick was personally involved in starting a number of churches in South Central Alaska. Anchorage City Church is one of them.
His passion is serving God and His people.

"All that we know today was first spoken into being by God Himself. He willed that it was recorded. He spoke and it was manifested. His Spirit continues to reverberate throughout His creation, as we resonate with His power and will, as we acknowledge that voice throughout eternity. Shouldn't that also be part of the record ?"

Rhon Duke
An ordained prophet,
In the late 1970's God began to use Rhon
to speak and minster through the Holy Spirit.
He and his wife Kit, reside in Anchorage, Alaska.

* * *

1 Timothy 1:18 (TPT)
So, Timothy, my son, I am entrusting you with this responsibility, in keeping with the very first prophesies that were spoken over your life, and are now in the process of fulfillment in this great work of ministry, in keeping with the prophecies spoken over you. with this encouragement use your prophesies as weapons as you wage spiritual warfare by faith and with a clean conscience.

Deborah has taken the responsibility of prophesies spoken over Alaska very seriously, spending innumerable hours scribing with tears and prayers, declarations and decrees as we have come together many times personally as well as with a group of leaders in our great state! Every state has a DNA, promises and a peculiar sound! As you read this handbook, you will begin to hear and see in a whole new level! I'm so honored and proud of one of Alaska's finest prophetic scribe, seer and watchmen- love Eleanor

Eleanor Roehl
Eleanor Roehl, (Nunapik: The Real Land) is Yupik Eskimo, from the
village of New Stuyahok, Alaska. She is a devoted wife to her husband

Robert for over twenty-eight years, a loving mom and co-owner of Eagles Nest Vacation Rentals in Kasilof, Alaska.
Eleanor is an author, and the founder of Alaska Declaration Link prayer movement.
She is also co-founder of Kingdom Warriors Alaska and Kingdom Alliance Network: an apostolic & prophetic ministry designed to activate multicultural Kingdom Leadership.
Eleanor has traveled throughout Alaska, the United States and Internationally, preaching, teaching, prophesying and flowing in the supernatural gifts of God.

* * *

"Life and death are in the power of the tongue." Words are very powerful and can shift the destiny of a nation. This excellent compilation of prophetic words spoken over Alaska will enable faithful intercessors to partner with God in declaring His will for the Great Land of Alaska. Our destiny lies before us. The great battle is at hand. Lift up your sword; release the shout; victory is ours!

Mary Glazier
Founder and President of Windwalkers International.
Mary is on the National Council for the U.S. Coalition of Apostolic Leaders
under the leadership of Apostle Joseph Mattera.
She is also a recognized leader with the Apostolic and Prophetic Elders led by Apostle Cindy Jacobs.
God has used Mary to raise up strategic intercessors and leaders in many nations.
Along with Robert and Eleanor Roehl, Mary co-founded Kingdom Alliance Network.
Mary is also on the Board of Directors for Intercessory Prayer Ministry, International.

Faithful, fiery and favored by God is my description of Deborah Rubey. She, like Anna the prophetess, was hidden away in the temple praying. But no, God has directed her to capture prophetic words given over the state of Alaska, pairing them with her prayers from the heart of God! The pages of this book ring with prophetic promise and cries of intercession-the prayers full of humility, forgiveness, and God's mighty power. She has gathered these powerful words of remembrance to be spoken over families, over this state and over the nation. God will unfold the destiny of this land as you join as one in decreeing these treasured prophetic declarations. There surely "will be a performance of those things promised by the Lord" as you speak out these words Deb has faithfully gathered.

Judith Green

A former teacher and ordained minister, has traveled the last 25 years, teaching and prophesying in 50 nations. She is a bible teacher and prophetic voice in Alaska, the United States and overseas. Her ministry, Voice to the Nations, also includes citywide and statewide strategic prayer, prophetic training and activation meetings, counseling and mentoring.
Judith has served on city reaching teams in the United States and other nations, on international apostolic leadership teams, international prayer teams,
mission teams and prophetic ministry teams.
Her heart's desire is that all would know the joy of Christ's presence in an intimate way,
to lift up His name and to lie in the overcoming power of the Holy Spirit.
Judith enjoys her two grown children and four grandchildren.

I just finished your book. What a gift of love and inspiration for the body of Christ in Alaska. I love that you have collected and scribed these precious, life giving prophecies for our remembrance. But more than that, I love the beautiful language of prayer that flows from your heart. You are one who is dear to the Father and faithful to remind Him of His word. You, like Mary, have pondered these words and treasured them in your heart.

This book affords opportunity for the body of Christ to unite in focused prayer for Alaska's destiny. May our prayers and declarations come before His throne as a fragrant offering, filling the bowls in heaven to overflowing. Lord Jesus, pour out your glory in Alaska.

Lorraine O'Neal
Lorraine is board president of Downtown Hope Center:
a homeless shelter for women and a center for the restoration of down-
trodden and destitute men and women, offering them the opportunity
for education, training and certification
from Hope's Culinary and Baking School,
Lorraine is also Anchorage Prayer Coordinator for National Day
of Prayer.
Lorraine resides in Anchorage Alaska with her
husband Eugene.

The following prophetic words printed within this book
were spoken by the indicated prophetic voice,
from around the United States,
as they spoke by the Spirit, over Alaska.
Most were scribed from an audio at a conference,
a meeting, or an individual recording.
One word was re-printed with his permission.
The prayers were composed by the author,
unless otherwise indicated.

Table of Contents

This Land is Mine

January 15, 1989 Mary Glazier

"Have I not spoken, saith the Lord, that I would pour out my anointing upon My Holy People; and if you could see what is taking place in the Spirit-

You would see strongholds falling around you...
You would see enemies fleeing before you...
You would see fear falling upon the enemy's camp because of your words...
You would see light penetrating dark areas that have been dark for generations...
You would see the Glory of the Lord rising upon your households...
You would see deliverance going forth from your mouth as your pray...
You would see violence coming down and scattering...
You would see darkness dissipating before the Presence of the Glory of the Lord upon the church of the living God

For yea, have I not led you into the land; and have I not opened doors before you; and have I not scattered the enemy from before you, saith the Lord. For the sword of the Lord is in your mouth; yea, even the Word of God is nigh thee, even in thy mouth, and you shall declare and it shall be done, saith the Lord. For I have given unto you a mouth filled with power and anointing. I have given unto you clothing pure and white. I have given unto thee the Sword of the Holy Ghost which is the Word of God.

And you will come against disease and it will flee from you
And you will come against bondage and it shall be broken
And you will come against injustice and there will be the faith and presence and justice of the Lord determined on that situation, saith the Lord.

For I have covered this land as My people have shouted from the mountains; as My people have shouted from the flatlands; and as My people have shouted from the rolling hills, so have I declared;
This land is MINE, saith the Lord, and I will take it unto Me and cover it with My Glory!"

ONE PRAYER

Oh, precious sovereign most High Lord,
we are so aware have You have divinely placed each of us in this land,
called Alaska.
For such a time as this.
We say in this time and in this new ERA of PEY, that we would use our
words You have given to us, and Your sword of Glory, which is Your
Word, which You have put within us, to invade the territory You have
given us to war for.

We declare that You have given us eyes to see and ears to hear and
hearts to heed.
We declare that the Land will hear the sound of the Glory of the Lord
coming across it, covering it with Your Goodness. *II Corinthians 3:17
says, where the Spirit of the Lord is, there is freedom.*
Causing disease to flee, injustices to fall, strongholds coming down,
and violence leaving this land because of Your presence. We trust Your
Word, as it is sealed in heaven, when You said You will give us the land
we tread upon.

And we war for this land called Alaska, to be filled with Your Glory.
We will fill the atmosphere with praise and worship and thanksgiving.
Causing darkness to flee across this great land. From one coastline to
another of Alaska, so that it seeps into the adjoined and nearby coun-
tries and attached lands.

And we declare this day, we will see heaven come to earth in Alaska,
across this vast state.

2

Fire in Alaska

January 6, 1991 Benny Hinn

"I see fire in Alaska, I see a fire in that whole western area of Canada and Alaska.
Alaska shall be inflamed with the glory of God. Now there is something interesting here, something interesting.

This is amazing, I don't know why. The Lord just said to me:

"The judgment coming on America will not affect Alaska because praying believers will protect Alaska from judgment."

TWO PRAYER

Father,

We humbly come before You, knowing it is not by might or by power, but by Your Spirit… You have said Lord.

You have called many in this state to pray, intercede, war, travail, dream, shout, dance, and stand in the gap for Your dream for Alaska.

Father, we ask that You give us strength for the day, that we don't grow weary in doing well. That we persevere with such a Holy Fire that is from You that no man, no circumstance of man, no situation of man, can put out this fire.

Set us on Holy fire Lord, for Your desire. That we would continue to press in, to pray, to war and battle for Your Kingdom come, Your will be done, in Alaska, as it has been determined before the beginning of time.

Raise up a mighty army of warring prayer soldiers in this hour, that would combat the enemy, not of our own skill or ability or strength, but empowered by You Lord.

We long to dream with You Lord, that Your fire spread across this Great Land.

3

Breaking Desolation

May 5, 1996 Chuck Pierce

"I have called this whole state for breaking desolation that has even encompassed those states that came from the beginning.
So, I say to you, see your season of war, that you might have the authority to break desolation.
And if you will take this authority, you will see reversal in the nation" saith the Lord.

So, I say to you,
"Begin to cause the reversal to come to the entire nation from Alaska"

THREE PRAYER

Father, You never leave us or forsake us. Your thoughts are higher than our thoughts, Your ways are higher than our ways.
Thank You Oh Lord, that You know our very ways.
Teach us Your ways, oh Lord.
We repent for the times we have embraced, unknowingly, this desolation. Thank You for Your forgiveness.

We know You will never abandon us, never leave us.
So, we come against the orphan spirit that has left so many in desolation, left so many feeling dejected and in a pit of depression, sadness, and loneliness. Only You can pull anyone out of that miry pit.

We speak into the state of Alaska right now, into the very atmosphere, from coast line to coast line, from border to border, from mountain top to each valley.
We declare the revelation of Sonship.
We declare the joy of the Lord,
the hope of our Lord,
the love of our Lord,
filling homes, streets, stores, streams and lakes. That joy be our portion and no more desolation.
We claim the abundance of all You have ever meant for us.

May we reflect Your love that is full of light that causes the darkness of desolation to flee.
We declare right now, the Light of Your Goodness and Love, spread across this great land, invading where desolation has tried to root itself.

Desolation - Webster dictionary
　　　　-Extreme sadness caused by loss of loneliness
　　　　-Grief, sadness, devastation, ruin
　　　　-Despondency, dejection, depression, sadness,

Gloominess, neglected, solitary without companion. Desolate is literally or figuratively "abandoned"

4

Apostolic Anointing

June 27, 1999 Cindy Jacobs

"The Lord is showing me that as Alaska comes into its anointing apostolically, it's going to affect all 50 states.

For the Lord says, I have positioned you in a position of authority. Satan has tried to oppress you, marginalize you Alaska, and push you down, because he has been very afraid of the apostolic authority I am giving to this state as a high place.

I see this crown of Alaska crowning the nations of the earth. I see this crown, and the Lord is showing me Esther's rising up, walking with the scepter of authority."

FOUR PRAYER

Oh, Lord, we are so humbled by how You have positioned this state. Forgive us, for being a people of dependence on ourselves. For it truly is You that we need. We trust, rely and depend upon You. By the renewing in the spirit of our mind, we put on our new self which in the likeness of God created in righteousness and holiness and truth, according to Ephesians.

We thank you Lord that You don't limit us. And we break off any limitation or marginalizing that the enemy has tried to put upon us, as a state. As a company of believers that are part of Your Bride, we thank You that we are strong and walk in the mighty power of Your Spirit.

We ask you to show us how to step even fuller, into this apostolic anointing that is on this state. We ask that those who are to rise up in this hour crowned in Your authority, not be delayed, not be sidetracked, not be distracted, but walk in Holy boldness, in the fire of Your presence.

We thank You for the call of the apostolic, to teach and train and equip and allow believers to operate effectively in the gifts of the Spirit. We ask You to show us how to not just operate effectively in this, as a state, but we desire to be one that brings what You have done in Alaska, to a Nation.

Even as Esther, Lord, thank You for such a time as this. We embrace this assignment in Alaska.

5

Alaska is a Redemptive Gift

2004 James Goll

"And because you are so strategic, Alaska is a redemptive gift of God to the entire United States! This was not an accident that this piece of territory was bought for such a cheap price! And God wants you to know that you are not a trinket that is just on the United States bracelet, you are not a trinket.

The Lord says: That you are a redemptive gift!
This state is a redemptive gift for the protection of the continental United States. This region is strategic, this region has the hand of God upon it. This region is blessed with a right conservative mindset, the Lord is going to bless that, and He's going to use that, and the military is going to be re-strengthened.

There are going to be resources. It is going to come from out of this region, because the Lord is going to raise up a plan, within a man, that the United States, even Canada will not be dependent upon OPEC for its oil. Because there are going to be resources, resources, resources, hidden resources, hidden resources, that are going to come forth from the land of the North and they shall be used during an hour of crisis, and there will be those who will have a forerunner anointing upon their life that will help network this thing into being."

FIVE PRAYER

Lord,

You knew before time, Your purpose for this state, Alaska.

You determined long ago regarding the purchase of Alaska, to be used as a kinsman redeemer for the rest of the United State of America.

Even as Boaz was kinsman redeemer for Naomi, and she got back all she had left and lost. And also in *Jeremiah 32*, the story of how the Jeremiah was used as a kinsman redeemer.

So also, we see as You have spoken, that Alaska is a redemptive gift to the United States.

We call forth the one You have raised and trained and prepared for this hour, the one with a plan, a strategy, method, design, for using the resources within this state. Those resources that have been covered and hidden, that You have reserved and planned to come forth in Your time. In the right time.

We call forth those who are purposed by Your divine plan to help connect and communicate Your design.

Keep us from being sidetracked from Your purpose.

Show us each our part in aligning with Your plan for Alaska to be at that Horaios time, which is, at the right time gate, for Your plan to unfold.

We long to walk out that which You have divinely purposed for this land.

No delay, and not too early, may we wait for Your lead, and may we always recognize it's not about us. But about Your Kingdom purpose and plan.

6

North to the Future

May 2016 Dutch Sheets

"Alaska has yesterday, today and tomorrow. All at the same time. In Alaska you can move forward into yesterday or you can move forward into tomorrow.

Tell my people to move forward into tomorrow, not yesterday."

SIX PRAYER

Lord, we thank You for yesterday. We thank You for what was, and the foundation of which You have had us build upon from yesterday.
We do want to move into the future, Into the now, according to Your plan.

Thank you, Holy Spirit, for flipping the switch that enables us to think differently, to know that an old cycle has been broken over this state Alaska.
We have left yesterday, and have moved into tomorrow.
We have moved into the new Era, we are moving in Spirit led thinking. With renewed minds. And enlarged hearts of Your love Lord.

There is rebuilding, reforming and taking the territory. We are going to eat what we didn't plant, we are going to reap what we didn't reap, because we are out of Egypt and into Canaan.
Our thinking is changed, our paradigm is changed and we are functioning and thinking differently. We are moving into tomorrow, we will not go back into yesterday.

The cycle that kept Alaska back is broken.

7

Alaska's Time

January 27, 2017 Eleanor Roehl

"The Spirit of the Lord is brooding across the land called Alaska, and there is an awakening in the hearts of My people, both near and far. I am meeting with them supernaturally, I am breathing into their very nostrils and I am opening up their eyes to see Me. I am opening up their ears to hear Me. Though they have not known Me, I say I am meeting with them, even in dreams and visions and they are knowing Me, they are coming into a knowledge of Me in a very supernatural way, in a very real and authentic way, and they will be coming to teach you and they will be coming to tell you about their dreams and their visions, for there is an awakening upon this land.

And I say upon this land there are many who are being birthed into a fivefold ministry, many who are being birthed into their calling and destiny, for I say that this is Alaska's time. This is Alaska's time and she shall come forth into her destiny and into her calling and into the original self that I have created her to be, long, long, long ago.

And I say that I am bringing into culmination of times, and I am going back and reaching back even into, its original time and purpose, and I am going back to the portals of time and I'm bringing those things that have been held back, and I say it is now. And I say I am establishing My kingdom order and My kingdom purpose for this land. Know that

I am taking this people by the hand and I am causing them to reach their inheritance, and they will know Me for who I really am. Not who they have heard about, not what they have read about, for I am meeting with them face to face. And yes, even those who have known Me for a very long, long time, I am breaking off that religiosity. I am breaking off that structure and legalistic spirit, and the pharisaical spirit that has held My people back and have oppressed them.

You will see many First Nations come with a raw sound, come with a raw sound from deep within. For this is Alaska's time for arising. There is an awakening and arising and moving forward for the groaning within My people and the groaning that is within the land.

For I say that my Ecclesia is rising and she is taking her place in Alaska and other nations."

SEVEN PRAYER

We say yes, to Your Kingdom order and Your Kingdom purpose for Alaska, Lord.

> *Romans 13:11 (tpt),"To live like this is all the more urgent, for time is running out and you know it is a strategic hour in human history. It is time for us to wake up! For our full salvation is nearer now than when we first believed"*

Thank You for what You have been forming within this land. Thank You for awakening the people of this land. Awakening into destiny callings. Awakening into destinies. And Arising. We thank You for restoring what had been held back, that You have kept this for now. For You are using Alaska to reach the end or final result of Your purpose for America.

We thank You, that You have heard the groanings, the travailing, the prayers and petitions of intercession and we thank You that they are being poured back into this state with Your divine purposes of the Ecclesia rising within Alaska.

We call forth even more dreams, visions and revelation for Your people of this state Lord. We call forth the first nations people of Alaska to arise and step into Kingdom action.

May we all come together as one new man.
We Praise Your Holy wonderful Name Jesus.

8

North to Alaska

March 8, 2017 Clay Nash

"This morning I awoke hearing- North to Alaska the rush is on. I saw the number 49 in a vision. I thought I was aware Alaska was the 49th state and verified this. I then heard the Lord speak 49 years ago. So, I looked up 1968. The North Slope discovery was discovered in 1968. Prudhoe is the English name but its French origin means Wiseman. The Strong's number 1968 in Hebrew means faithful and in Greek means to fall into ones embrace. Also, the Strong's number 49 means expiation or atonement.

Now this is what God is saying:

There is about to be a North Slope discovery of Holy Spirit oil that will release a movement that will bring forth the wise ones of Alaska to form a solidarity of leaders needed to allow the State of Alaska to step into its significant and key role leadership of this nation.

The Lord is saying: Lean into faithfulness of My embrace that is filled with empowering grace, that will cause a movement of expiation releasing healing to the land and causing it to give up even greater treasures from the land.

The Lord says: Watch out for the Wyatt Earp and Tex Rickard's that will come to line their own pockets and build their own ministry from the Holy Spirit of oil release of endued power.

Judge and cast not stones."

EIGHT PRAYER

Oh Father, the plans and purposes You destined long ago for Alaska have been unfolding over time. We receive what has been and what will be, according to Your purpose and Your desire.

We say bring it on Lord, the Holy Spirit oil, that will flow through this state.

We call forth those leaders, those wise ones, those with Kingdom wisdom, ones that will have unity with each other, those that will operate in one accord, for Your dream for Alaska. We pray protection around them, we ask for great revelation and open portals of Your kingdom over them. We call them out of the caves and into the forefront of your plan.

We say, Alaska will lean into faithfulness. To You Lord will be our loyalty, for You are the one we trust, rely and depend upon. We call forth the faith mentioned in *Hebrews 11*, into Alaska. For we know that faith is the assurance in what we hope for, the conviction of things not seen. We hold fast the confession of our hope without wavering, for You who promised is faithful.

We want faith to spark courage across this land and cause mighty warriors to arise.

We thank You that You embrace us, and we lean into Your embrace of empowering grace, that releases healing into this land. Causing the land to open up and uncover hidden resources.
Not just for this state but for this Nation.

Thank You for the spirit of discernment as we move forward in this.

9

Healing Army Arise

August 31, 2017 Chuck Pierce

"I called this land for healing, for there is an anointing for healing in this land, not just for the land to be healed, but the anointing for healing in this land called Alaska.

And I say it will run like a raging river, down south and to the east, saith the Lord.
I say to you, it will begin to flow outward, just as the garden had a river of healing flowing through it.

This land will be known as that which flowed out with healing for distinct nations, even Europe will know of the healing that comes forth from Alaska.

So, I say to you: I am unblocking the healing anointing in this land and a healing army will arise".

NINE PRAYER

Oh, Mighty One, Oh Great and powerful One, we have heard of the healing wave coming our way for so many years. Many have had dreams and visions of this wave of healing coming into the state.
You have been showing us this wave, this river, this stream of healing, that is part of Your plan for this land called Alaska.

We call forth this healing anointing. We say rise out of the land, and those in the land that carry this, we say begin to steward this gift with great boldness.
I Corinthians 12:9 says: To another faith by the same Spirit, to another the gift of healing by the same spirit...

We say and agree- It is not by might or by power or anything we can do or say, it is by Your Spirit.

Lord, let Alaska be one to carry this anointing well. That Your name be glorified.

That this anointing of healing, this gift of healing, this presence of Your healing will flow throughout this land and past the borders of this mighty State of Alaska.

That nations be healed and Your name be lifted High. That others know, You are God, and there is no other.

In Jesus Name
Amen and Amen...

10

Overcoming Spirit in this Land

August 31, 2017 Mary Glazier

"Alaska is coming into something brand new. The 150th anniversary of our purchase from Russia, a triple jubilee. An amazing new identity falling on our land. And as you warriors standing in the gap do not faint, God has given us a theme.

The whales that come up from the bottom of the ocean, even as Jonah was in the belly of the whale, as it were as a place of death and darkness and yet at the word of the Lord, when his heart was fainting inside of him, he began to rise because God heard his cry. God hears the cry of Alaska. He hears your cry and you are coming up from the bottom of the depth.

And the Lord says: There is a new hour upon this land, for I have called out across this land, who will take a stand for me against the evil doers, who will rise for me against those who work iniquity.

I have called Alaska to the forefront in this hour, for there rests upon this land a resurrection anointing and you will come up from the depths and you will bring your sound with you, and your eyes will be fixed upon the King, and the heavens will shake.

For the Lord says:

"I am bringing down the territorial spirit, his reign ends now, he will no longer hold your land bondage, he will no longer hold your people in bondage, but chains are beginning to fall and prison doors are beginning to open and those that have been afar off will come near and those that once knew the King, will know Him once again, and they will not turn back.

And from the bottom of the ocean will come those that rise up with new identity, saith the Lord. And they will rise up with a new joy, and the enemy will not prosper against them, for the Lord has sent the sound of His voice ahead of His army, and there is coming an overcoming Spirit to this land and chains fall, the darkness lifts,

And the Glory will rest upon the State of Alaska once again."

TEN PRAYER

Father, we thank You that You have never forgotten us, or forsaken us, even when we have been low and weary and in a dark place.

We thank You that You are strengthening the intercessors and the warriors who have been standing in the gap for this land, for your Kingdom purposes, for years and years.
We thank You that You have heard the cry coming from this land. That You inclined Your ear to hear.

We ask for ears to hear this new sound, in this new time. This brand-new Era, we know You are moving and performing, something You have never done before.
The sound that is from Your Kingdom we wish to release with resurrection anointing, causing life to spring up in Alaska, where there has been darkness. We ask, You to send the sound Lord, that will awaken the prodigal to Your voice. That there will be many rising up in strong and courageous strength, and be overcomers.

For *John 16: 33 says, You overcame the world.* And in *1 John 4:4, it says we are of God and greater is He in us than he that is in the world.*

We press on to walk in that overcoming spirit.
In that place where we will prevail by the Spirit, where we stand upon, on top of, that which has kept us down in the past, and now chains are falling and darkness is lifting.

Let Your Glory Lord, be what rests upon this state.

11

Deliverance for a Nation

August 31, 2017 Chuck Pierce

"And the Lord says: There is a communication line being established new and fresh from this territory, from its original people that He put here. That the voice of those people is going to start allowing the voice of God to rise up, and be communicated throughout the entire nation.

That's how deliverance will come to a nation.
For the whole land is coded from north, all the way into the entire lower portions of America. And sorrow and trail of tears, that have gone before the ashes that have occurred. That has not stopped Gods word that is held within the bone marrow that he has coded into this nation.

And the Lord says: He is getting ready to unlock the code of victory in this Nation.
And the unlocking starts in Alaska."

ELEVEN PRAYER

Oh Jesus, Jesus, Jesus, how we need You.
How we hunger for Your leading, for Your direction for Your wisdom.
It is through You and to You and in You are all things.

We know it is by You oh Lord, that this new way of communication will be brought to the surface. That which has been reserved and hidden for this time. We call it forth Lord, that the peoples of this land will come forth with this new sound.

That this coding that is in the land be unlocked and opened, and be loosed into this Great State of Yours, and into the Nation of America.

That the mystery in the history of Alaska, that has been covered, and held back, be opened and unlocked as we move forward into this Era.

Lord, let us not hold tight to what isn't just for us, let us have Your wisdom and Your knowledge and Your strategy on how to move in this, for Your Kingdom come, Your will be done, in Alaska , in America, as it is in heaven. Amen

Communication – Webster Dictionary

-the act or process of using words, sounds, signs, or behaviors to express or exchange information or to express your ideas, thoughts, feelings. Et

-the ways of sending information to people by using technology

Unlock – *open, to make something available. To be loosed.*

Code – *a system of signals or symbols for communication.*
-a system of principles or rules, moral code

12

The Shaking

August 31, 2017 Chuck Pierce

"The Glory shaking begins in Alaska.
He said: You will be known as the state where the Glory shaking began.

Will you shake physically? Probably.
You will shake, but it won't end with Alaska.
It will penetrate right down in through the western coast and it will miss California, and it will head across in through Oklahoma in through Missouri, and all the way into the Carolinas.

The Lord says: The shaking that begins here in Alaska, the Glory shaking, will cross a Nation and cause a Nation to come alive.

Get ready for the Glory shaking to begin.
The shaking this time, is going to be a people shaking, because there is Glory within the people of this state, that God is ready to shake loose. The shaking will go on in the realignment of Gods people in this state. And He starts shaking and says the first thing He is going to shake off of you, any and all discouragement that has gotten on you from past season. Stand up and shake that off.

You have lost sight of what you are here to steward.

You're going to become the Kingdom stewards that become the model for an entire nation.

Shake loose Kingdom stewardship.

Then He says this:

I have called you to be the Seers of an entire nation. And I'm going to shake loose your ability to see in a realm that no one else in this nation can see.

And I'm going to give you access in communication that you didn't have in the past.

And even thought at one point, 'this is it'.

But the Lord says: You ain't seen anything yet, because the access of communication that I'm going to give you will astound a nation."

TWELVE PRAYER

Oh Lord, who can describe Your Glory, oh my God, what does Your Glory sound like, what does Your Glory look like?
Lord, You have shown many traits of Your Glory, of Your character, Your attributes, of who You are.

We ask that we recognize the shaking You are doing in this state, that we don't try and analyze and put it in a category, but we embrace Your Glory Shaking. The shaking that will bring a realignment of Your people in this state.

The shaking that frees, that is purposed to bring to us to a specified place in You, in Your Glory.
We desire to be Kingdom stewards for You. Show us how to steward Lord, Holy Spirit teach us, mentor us, counsel us. Give us an anointing to steward well.

Thank You, You have given us spiritual eyes to see. Increase our vision Lord. Stretch out the tent pegs of our vision Lord. Give us that panoramic view, that zoom view, that wide view, that deep view, that which You have called us to see.

We ask, that we begin to see and hear and walk in the new communication You have for Alaska, we call that forth Lord, for Your Kingdom purpose, that the Nation will know You.

In Your Glory, there is no discouragement, no desolation, no sickness, no darkness, only Your presence.

Shake us Lord, shake us, till this country shakes with Your Glory.
Shake us and launch us Lord, we choose to walk in cadence with You.

13

Crowning of Alaska

February 7, 2018 Eleanor Roehl

"I am crowning Alaska with my love, I am crowning Alaska with my peace that passes all understanding, for her days of wilderness are over and the Shunamite women is running, the Shunamite woman is running, the Church and the Ecclesia is running to take her place, and no longer will she be hiding in shame, but I say now, she is taking her rightful place in My Kingdom and I say that those that have, the enemy that has tried to toy and tried to ploy with My Church is being cast down, for there is a new crown that I am setting upon the State of Alaska."

THIRTEEN PRAYER

Jesus, oh Jesus, beautiful Jesus, Your name never fails. Your name is powerful. We declare the name of Jesus over Alaska this day.

You are crowning Alaska with a new authority in this season. We hunger for Your love Lord. We recognize that without Your love we would be clanging symbols. We hunger and know we need Your peace to walk out this new Era we are now in.

That even as the Shunamite women went running for the one she knew could help her, so also, we run to You, You are the One we focus on. You are the only One that can raise us up. You are the only One that can bring life to the dry places, to the places of shame, You bring healing and hope as You break off guilt and regret, dishonor and disgrace. For we are Your people, and we thank You for the weapons of our warfare are not carnal, but mighty in God for pulling down strongholds.

We recognize You have called us to steward what You are doing in Alaska in this time. We long to be faithful and true, with integrity and with Kingdom purpose as we move forward.

We say, Yes, to the gift of stewarding Your grace and peace and love, that You have put upon Alaska.

14

Special Mantle

June 19, 2018 Stephen Powell

"This is a birthing state. There are midwife angels in this state.

For the Lord says: This truly is a state where things begin and where things end.
And the Lord says: If you want to be something that foreruns something, if you want to be one of that pioneers something, if you want to be one beginning something, you have to have courage at times to end something.

To say "NO" to put a stop to something, to say "NO" we are not moving in that, "NO" we are going to move with the Lord. It takes boldness saints, it takes boldness. Everybody's doing it, so, so, so, what is God telling you to do?
You are not like every other state in the union, if you haven't noticed. You have a special call. A special mantle

I see arthritis, I see the Spirit, the bones of strength of the apostles and prophet's foundation, there has been like a crippling that has come in, and the Lord is saying: I am coming with some fresh oil.

Some of you got to get moving.

The Lord is saying: There is some of you that He wants to recapture momentum with, He wants to recapture momentum with.

Some of you need to get conditioned to move in the Lord.
The Lord does not operate at man's pace, the Lord doesn't operate at the pace of the church."

FOURTEEN PRAYER

Oh Lord, how we love You, how great is Your faithfulness to all generations.

How mighty are Your wonders, for You alone are worthy to be praised and exalted.

We thank You for this great state of Alaska where You have placed us. It is not by chance each of us are here. For You have a plan and purpose and a destiny for each one.

And as You have called this state a birthing state, one that something originates in, and begins in, we ask that we know how to cooperate with these angels You have here to bring forth the birthing.

We ask for Your guidance in creating new ideas and methods as You use us to forerun, and pioneer something new for Your Kingdom. Pull it out of us Lord!

We ask that by Your strength we be strong and courageous. That we have a Holy discernment to know when to say yes, and when to say no. We want to walk in that special mantle you have on Alaska, this place of authority from You, not our own, but Yours Lord. You receive all the Glory.

We ask for that fresh oil, to bring about momentum where there has been a stiffness and a holding back. We ask You to forgive us for being passive and not moving, that has caused delay. We say, no more delay Lord. Your Holy Oil is coming upon us. We will move forward into Your plans.

We will get before You and fill up with Your oil daily, we don't want to be caught unaware.

We say we choose You Lord.

15

Spirit of Forgiveness

September 12, 2018 Negiel Bigpond

"I saw Alaska as the head of everything, that Alaska will be releasing many, many things, I see things just flowing out of those mountains, out of the lights, out of the water ways, releasing.
And what I see was a time and a gift of forgiveness.

Alaska, you carry that true forgiveness.
I believe it will come out of Alaska, the Spirit of Forgiveness, it's like a cloud, I see a cloud, like the northern lights, its bright and brilliant, and it begins to flow and move, it's like a storm, that's calm and calms the land. The act of excusing or pardoning someone.

Forgiveness is an act of pardoning someone.
The act of forgiveness will release punishment, a good release.

Holding unforgiveness punishes oneself."

FIVETEEN PRAYER

Oh, heavenly Father, how we need You. We repent for our unforgiveness towards our sisters and brothers. Forgive us for holding any resentment or jealousy towards them, open our eyes to see what we are operating out of, what we are filtering our words and thoughts through. That we might see and repent and know Your marvelous kindness, that we might walk in Your miracles of mercy that You have poured out for all of us.

Father, may we all walk carefully, as You have called us all in this hour. May our leaders, those who are called to leadership in this hour, be ones to operate in Your love which is so mighty.

Your word in *Mathew 6:14 says if we forgive men, You will forgive us.*

We ask for Holy Spirit to speak strongly, loudly and interrupt us when we forget this.

May the anger towards others, of jealousy, blaming, resentment, be broken off this state.

Let Your Spirit of forgiveness bring us the gift of repentance with forgiveness, falling on this land, bringing healing and unity.

16

The Violence of My Love

September 15, 2018 Linda Hiedler

"He said: I am about to release the reality of the violence of My love. You have called Me to take you to a deeper place in My love and it's not what you think, it will be like the strength of a hurricane, it will be shaking of an earthquake, like surgery, where you say, I have been saved, because He took His violent love and did not hold back to cut away the thing that was holding me back, the thing that would have caused my death. He loved me violently enough to take it.

And part of this with the flood, and the seeing all this washed away, He said: There is a violence when that happens, but He said: You will see that it is the strength of My love.
He said: Look at the hurricane that has just come thru, and imagine a shackle trying to stand up against that.
But the violence of My love comes in, it will do what I am sending it to do, it will break chains,
it will tear down old structures,
it will cleanse away old things,
it will shake the path so that you are able to walk in a straight path after that.

He said: Receive, the violence of My love, it may not appear to be My love when it first hits you, especially if you're expecting My love to be very comforting and soft and quiet.

So, I want you to know I am coming with a violence, a violence, a violence of My love that it will do what I am sending it to do and after it, you will say,

Lord, thank You for loving me enough to let me experience the violence of Your love."

SIXTEEN PRAYER

Oh, My Glorious Father, You are full of love. It's just who You are, full of mercy and truth and grace and power. You have heard our cry unto You for years now, calling on Your love. We so need Your love, for each other and for the world. Your word says it is by our love for each other that the world will know You. We have been seeking You, we have been seeking Your love, Lord.

We thank You, that You know when we can handle or steward Your love in a kingdom way. And we thank You for preparing us for this violent love of Yours, that will take out of each of us anything which has had a grip on us and held us back from moving forward into You more fully.

We long to be ready to embrace the strength of Your love, the force and great energy of Your love, Your love that breaks chains, tares down walls, cleanses and heals, and straightens our walk.

Isaiah says, Your word oh Lord does not go forth empty, without accomplishing what You desire, and without succeeding in the matter for which You sent it.

We wait on You for Your performance Lord.

Thank You for ears to hear, eyes to see and a heart to heed, when You move.

17

Occupy, Occupy, Occupy

October 19, 2018 Heather Ramert

"I hear the Lord saying: I have land deeds for you. These deeds are paid in full. There is spiritual land and natural land. These are positions that you have stepped on and off of. And positions that He is opening up for the first time ever in your life.

He said: My son, my daughter, don't you know I saw you in that battle on the land, and you won victory? You don't know, and you thought you failed. You stepped back and said I'm sorry Lord. And I say, My daughter, My son, you have had many victories! Ah, while waiting you have been sidelined, the Lord has said: I have been fighting your battles, and I have prepared the land for you. This land in your family, this is favor, this is land in your job and there is not lack".

The Lord is saying: Step into those places. The Lord is saying: No fear of man any longer, no lack will meet you, because I have provision for you.

We have a divine partnership says the Lord, out of *Ephesians 3:20, "God can do immeasurable more than we can ask or imagine, according to his power at work in us through His Spirit!*
The Lord says occupy, occupy, occupy this land!

I am opening new doors with My goodness, it is the wine flow.

And as acts of old in the apostles that rose up the generous spirit, the acts of the apostles bubbled up, also, and there will be relics on the land that you will see, relics that have negative connotations to them, they will be people even, that you will see, and you will see the redemptive quality in these new, old relics.

There's a positive quality My children will see and the Lord says: Occupy with my goodness.

It's going to saturate the land and bring these things up, and many will taste and see that the Lord is good."

SEVENTEEN PRAYER

Oh Father, You are the best treasure of them all. How You are towards us, we cannot even wrap our mind around Your goodness and greatness and Your love.

We thank You for how You have given us natural land, and restored back what was meant to be. And how You will continue to restore and redeem. For it is who You are, Great and Mighty Redeemer.

And we thank You for the spiritual land that You have for us to occupy. You have these deeds and instruments, sealed and containing legal transfer for Your Body in Alaska.

Give us eyes to see and the paradigm to understand what we are seeing.

That which once seemed negative from the past, show us the new and redemptive quality of these. Show us that mystery from the past that has yet to be revealed as fine treasure.

Your word says in *Mat 13:52, that those who have become disciples of the Kingdom of Heaven are like a head of household and will bring out of his treasure things new and old.*

Forgive us for passing over and disregarding that which is reserved for now, that which was and is to be now.

Show us Lord, we are dependent on You to open our eyes to these mysteries. That we might occupy this land Alaska in Your mercy, Your kindness, Your favor and Your goodness.

For Your loving kindness endures forever...

We decree this across this Great Land, called Alaska.

Occupy- Webster dictionary.

    -To fill or be in.

    -To engage the attention or energies of

    -To take up

    -To take or hold possession or control of

    -To reside in as an owner or tenant

18

Alaska is Being Born Again

October 19, 2018 Eleanor Roehl

"He said: Alaska is being born again, He said: Alaska is being born again. Alaska we are being born again.

He says: I am bringing you through your re-birthing state, no longer will you have still-births as it were, premature births or your promises stolen, but you are bringing forth that with I have placed within your very DNA, within your very blood line, within the land, there are promises in the land, you know I am talking spiritual.

God has a plan and a purpose specific for Alaska
I have placed within your DNA My promises, He said

Alaska is being born again, He is birthing within us new dreams, new hopes, new vision.
Get ready for the suddenlies.

The Lord say: Our land is pregnant, it is pregnant with recourse and it is getting ready to come forth in His timing and His way. And the government, the state or man's hand will not corrupt it, because He has made us wise stewards. He is placing the right ones at the helm of different things for the recourses to be developed properly and not for man's selfish gain.

Then He said: The atmosphere in Alaska is pregnant, it's pregnant with HIS glory."

EIGHTEEN PRAYER

Father, oh Holy One, You know the beginning, the end, and all that is between.
For You see all things, and You created all things.
All things are for Your Glory.
Alaska is for Your Glory.

Thank You that You are bringing Alaska into a place of Kingdom people that become real and develop a greater direct and personal relationship with You, those that draw from You daily and walk with You hourly.

You are causing Alaska to be re-born. Thank You that You have stilled the still-births, that those dreams You plan will not be born dead any longer. Or be out of timing, not too soon or too late.

You are a promise keeper. And the promises You put in this land are Yours that You will keep. Those promises that are in the very DNA of Alaska. That You planned from creation.

Open our spiritual eyes, Lord, to embrace and run with new dreams, new hopes and new vision.
Your word says in *John 3:7, that one must be born again*, re-birth Alaska Lord for your Kingdom purposes. To fulfill all You destined this great Land to accomplish.

We don't know which way the wind is blowing, but we can hear it. Open our ears Lord. We long to hear You moving, to hear the sound You make as you move across this land.
As you re-birth Alaska.

We declare this day, Alaska is a Glory State.

19

Come up Higher

October 9, 2018 Mary Glazier

"For there are wars and rumors of war everywhere on the right, and on the left, yet the Lord would say to you: My Spirit is hovering over My Kingdom Church.
And, the church in Alaska will rise up to her full potential.
For I have determined an outpouring of the Spirit and will visit this state and shake the land from the north to the south.
I will give you the right leadership, ask of me, I will position the right leadership for you, and I will put into place the right policies for you and I will answer your cry for this land.

I am putting my anointing on this land and as you walk your land, as you pray for your land, as your cry out, I will move on your behalf saith the Lord, for there are riches in the land that are yet to be redeemed, there are riches in this land that will yet come to the forefront saith the Lord. There are riches in my people in this land that have yet to find the fullness of their destiny.

I'm calling you up higher tonight saith the Lord, I will do this thing for you, you will not be left out, you are not alone, my eye is on every single one of you and I know your destiny.
I know your path and I know the love I have in my heart for you, come together as one, lift up your voice as one, for your ear, the ear of your

Father inclined unto you this night and I hear the cry on every one of your hearts tonight, saith the Lord."

NINETEEN PRAYER

Father, thank You for Your Word, thank You that You tip us off on things to come.

Your word says You don't do anything without revealing it to the prophets first.
Mathew 24:6 tells us *we will hear of wars and rumors of wars.*
Eccl 3:8 says *there is a time for war*, and You have equipped Alaska for this war.
We are calling in those that are of Your choosing for this time, for this assignment, ones that will lead in righteousness and lead for You, not for man. We ask You Lord, to pull them into their assignment.

Thank You that You have heard the cry coming from this land, the many years of many walking the land, crying out, declaring and decreeing Your promises over this land.

Show us how to come alongside You and work with Your Spirit and the anointing that You have poured into this land. And into the rich people of this land.
Those that You destined to be here then and now. That as they cried out in faith, believing your word over this land, they believed and faith sparked courage within them and they became mighty warriors, raising up others.

We step up higher Lord, in Your strength, and Your power and Your anointing. Quicken us by Your Holy Spirit, to put aside our separateness and gather in one accord. With Your purpose and Your dream and Your plans for Alaska. That we encourage each other and build each other up in You.

20

New Sound

December 18, 2018 Heather Ramert

"God has released this new sound Alaska is hearing. Alaska is hearing and they are listening in a different way. Alaska is listening in a different way and Alaska is responding in a different way. There is a response that is different from leaders on down.

The Lord showed me a picture of Jesus above the state of Alaska. And we know Him as crowned with many crowns, and this was a two-fold vision. But this last vision was where I saw Jesus and He was holding a crown and there was crown on His head, and there were crowns around His feet. He was in a heavenly realm over Alaska, but beams of light shone like wagon wheel spokes out over Alaska from all direction from each of those crowns.

He's crowned with many crowns, the crown of mercy, the crown of righteousness, the crown of love, the crown of redemption the crown of salvation , the crown of a redeemer, the crown of the Son of God, the crown of the Son of Man, the crown of righteousness, again.

When we come into agreement, the Lord says: Yes, the staking, there's agreement. We have come into agreement with the crown of authority in heaven in the heavenly realms and it comes down into our state.

We come into agreement here, we humbled ourselves here, we've removed ourselves here…

The light shines in the darkness and there is movement and we are responding in a new way."

TWENTY PRAYER

Our Father, who is in heaven, Hallowed and Holy is Your name.

Oh, how we are so in awe of Your goodness and Your power and Your might and Your wisdom and Your love. It's just who You are.
And how You purposed each one of us, with a destiny.
You created Alaska with a purpose and a destiny assignment to fulfill Your kingdom purpose.

Thank You, Lord, for the new sound, thank You Lord that Alaska is hearing differently. That You are shifting paradigms and we are hearing unlike before. Help us as we hear unusual and special things we have not heard before, and that we align our hearing with Your heart.

We love You Jesus, we worship You Jesus, You have victory, power, honor , glory and authority in this Land of Alaska. As you are the Light of the world, and You pour out Your Life-Giving Light over this land and this people, we say Yes Lord, Yes.

We know without Your light we would be like in a dungeon in darkness wandering with no destination. But Your light shines and is the light to our path. Glory, Glory, Glory.

Teach us Holy Spirit how to walk in this authority, that You have crowned Alaska in, and that You have called Alaska to walk in.

With our hearts low before You Lord, we say…
Let Your will be done as it is in heaven as we watch for Your performance in this Land for Your kingdom purpose.

21

Great Change Coming

February 23, 2019 Eleanor Roehl

"For there is a great change coming upon the Land, and the economy of Alaska.

There is great change coming on the horizon.

And I say to you: Prepare yourselves, for the change is at hand upon the land.

This great land that has been seemingly far and foreign to so many will now become something that would become even a fancy to many.

For many will come from foreign lands, many will come on the tourist boats, and on air, and on land, and they will come and they will taste and see not only what I am doing in the natural, but what I am doing in the spiritual, for there are hard changes but there are also fruitful changes.

So I say: Even those who live off the land, prepare yourselves for there is change coming to the land, there are resources that will be developed, some good and some very difficult.

You will begin to see a downturn in the economy for a bit. But there will be an uptick and it will grow and it will grow fast.

I say: Even to the watchmen and the intercessors, stay on the wall, and begin to pray , not just for the borders of Alaska, but for the streets of Alaska. And I say: To the hub towns of Alaska.

Begin to pray, come together, and begin to declare and decree the prophetic words spoken over your land and over your people. For there is much clashing that you will begin to see and fighting for position and fighting over territories and over streets to gain control.

But I say: Church rise up, rise up as one, rise up as one, and begin to wage a good warfare over the prophesies that have been spoken over , not just the four walls of your building, but over this great land.

For this great land will be known not only for her riches and resources, but this great land will be known for My Glory and the manifestation of My Glory on many levels.

So, take heed, take warning, take this time to prepare yourselves and begin to fight the good fight for this is much to be won."

TWENTY-ONE PRAYER

Oh Father, You who formed this earth and everything in it. You who created us, man and women, You, who own the resources and the land. For from You and to You are all things.

Give us wisdom in the preparing. Show us how to make ourselves ready for something You will be doing, to make ready for activity, purpose and use. Give us Your wisdom Lord. Let us be ones that have ears to hear what the Spirit has to say, that we don't get sidetracked, but stay focused.

We call forth those who would steward wisely the hidden resources within this land, those that would manage and tend and oversee that which You assign to them, those that would not be corrupt or for their own gain, but would walk in integrity and honor. That the resources and this great land bring glory to Your name.

We ask You to send Your angels to encourage the watchmen and the intercessors, that they not grow weary or downcast, but remain on assignment. Let there be a re-firing, reigniting of a holy fire that cannot be contained by man or man's plans, upon the watchmen in this hour, that they hear from heaven and pray Your will be done. Expand their hearing Lord, and let them begin to hear those things going that cannot be heard with natural hearing, for Your Kingdom purpose.

May all be moved to call upon You, as in *I Timothy 2*, with declaration, decrees, and petitions, thanksgivings, praying at all times.

May we all find our tribes and gather, as we know there is an anointing and strength in the cluster. That we learn how to war together, pray together, live together in one accord.

As we wait to see your performance of many levels of your Glory come forth in Alaska.

22

A New Movement

March 19, 2019 Judith Green

"The Spirit of the Lord is speaking to me and I am seeing a move over the State of Alaska.

I've never seen this kind of movement, He is moving so low to the ground that He is separating between the ground we walk on, and the people that are walking on the ground. He's inserting Himself, He Says: I'm underneath and loosing these paradigms and old habits and old actions that Alaska has operated in, because this is a new day.

He says He's preparing a flexibility, of moving out of an old place, into a new place, behold old things have passed away, all things have become new.

He even says: There is a new way of hearing that is coming before us. It is right in front of our eyes. It is like His voice comes right in front of our eyes and in front of our hearts. "Because this is the day of the hearts", says the Spirit of God.

He says: There is a great touching of heart. And the movement is to prepare for a day, even the animals. He said: I can see the animals scurrying around they are aware that shift has come.

He said: Hidden things are going to be uncovered and they are not just bad things that are to be uncovered and exposed, they were finances hidden that were coming to the surface and being revealed.

He said: Groups are going to start forming, and He even called them action committee's or action groups that are going to be coming together, not action groups politically, necessarily, I know that it is not them, but it is action groups in the Spirit, He said.

He said: we are going to begin to see break outs, He said: All of the sudden there will be a group that is meeting together and there will be a break out in the group that movement will take place, it will separate, and the new will come in and there will be a new way of seeing and not just declarations, but there are actions that they will be doing in the Spirit and these things will be miraculous things.
They are going to be miraculous divisions, between hope and hopelessness, miraculous between want and financial provision, miraculous division between walking in the natural and walking in the Spirit.

God says: He is shifting the land and we are to dive right in and make that declaration."

TWENTY-TWO PRAYER

We worship You Lord, we exalt You Lord, we lift up Your name. Let the name of the Lord be exalted in this State of Alaska. Let the name of the Lord be lifted and exalted in our lives.

We love the way You speak, and the way You uncover hidden treasures that have been reserved for now. We thank You for the new movement, the new change of place or position and change of posture that is on Your people in Alaska, and in the atmosphere.
We thank You that You are loosing paradigms, those ways of thinking about and those ways of how we have done things for so long. We receive Your changes Lord. Thank you for renewing our minds. Help us walk this out, getting in your Word and in Your presence, where we are transformed, from Glory to Glory. Thank You for the flexibility from You to move easily, breaking into a new place.

Oh Lord, expand our hearing, may we be attentive to the slightest sound or movement from You. May we incline our hearts to You in this time during this shift when You are wanting us and calling us to change positions and directions. Let our eyes be on You to hear and see this sound Lord. Your word talks about being able to see the way the wind blows, so may our eyes be wide open to see the way Your Spirit blows and moves and leads and directs.

Let the Spirit guide us, and may we be attentive to the guiding of Your Spirit, leading and directing and forming committees and groups appointed for specific functions, for Your Kingdom purpose.
We say yes, to this and yes to You. May we steward the purposes of these groups, becoming productive in activity for You, in whatever way You choose, for Your purpose for Alaska and beyond.

We declare today as an announcement: There has been a shift in Alaska, there has been a movement in this land. There is and will be miraculous separations out of what is Holy and what is unholy, what is clean and what is unclean.

For Your Kingdom and Your plans and Your dream for this land Alaska, and the people You have in this land.

23

Multiplication

July 30, 2019 Judith Green

"The Lord says: This is the time of multiplication, into the state of Alaska. And that I will multiply resources for ones that need to be hidden will remain hidden for a time, and the ones that need to be exposed will be exposed that are good for the land.
This is the time of multiplication of produce says the Lord.
Of multiplication of finances and multiplication of goods in the land.
It will be a time of multiplication for people.

For I am coming into people's hearts and multiplying My Glory and multiplying My Presence and I am sweeping My arms out to draw unto Me those that have been lost and those who have been cast aside.

For I am multiplying the people of the kingdom in this land, and in every way. I will multiply. You watch for it, I am going to bring in an awareness that this is a time of bounty, a time of goodness, a time of provision.

Do not quickly judge when something comes to the surface and say this is not good, this is bad. Rather say to Me: Is this one You are exposing, or one that You want me to agree with? Then make agreement with Me, says the Lord.

Make agreement with Me and call forth those things that I'm exposing but allow to be hidden, those things that I have My hand over and capped for this time."

TWENTY-THREE PRAYER

Our Father, who is in heaven, we come before You, with hungry hearts, anticipating hearts, expecting hearts, eager hearts, lifting You up, for Your Kingdom purpose in this state.

Lord Your word says in *Luke 12:2 that there is nothing covered up that won't be revealed and hidden that will not be known.*

We thank You that You are uncovering many things in this era. We thank You that You have chosen Alaska for multiplication of things in the natural and the spiritual.

Even as in *Ezekiel 36,* where You poured out multiplication on Israel, so also You are doing within Alaska, and just like for Israel, it is not just for us, but for Your Name, that a nation may know that You are Lord.

Lord, You have equipped us for now, and are equipping us for what You are bringing into Alaska.

May we not be quick to form an opinion about something or someone, but we want to process through You and through Your Holy Spirit, as not to make wrong judgements.

We call in those prodigals and those who have been outcast and we thank You that those prayers for them have been heard for years.
You are pouring out Your goodness into the land and into the people of Alaska.

We say, we align with You and Your purpose Lord. Help us, for we are dependent upon You. May we not to let our own agenda get in the way. Let us see clearly, let us hear with clarity. Increase our discernment. We intentionally look to You.

Spring up oh well, Spring up oh well... that which has been reserved for this hour.

24

Holy Spirit, Holy Friend

August 8, 2019 Marty Cassidy

"I was in *Acts 2*, and I heard the sound, and I felt the wind, and I saw the fire. And I knew Holy Spirit was going to hit and come in a way. And I kept saying Lord, what does this mean? Because during that experience the minute I got thru the *Acts 2*, I heard, Holy Spirit say: Now its *Revelation 22*.

And I knew exactly what the Lord was trying to say to me, I just didn't know when, when to loose the word. I have carried it for a year.

Today Alaska the Lord says to you:
You are the upper room, you are the upper room.
He says: I am coming in a power with My Spirit and I'm going to breath on you a whole new way.
I'm going to loose a new Pentecost.
And He says: What your response is to be, is to say
"Even so come", the Bride and the Spirit say "Come".
I call you as the uppermost of the state, the upper room, that place called to birth a new Pentecost over this nation, over this land.

And He says: I'm going to show you new characteristics of this person, this third person of the Godhead, He's the one in the earth realm, He's the One in you.

He's said you're going to be calling Him Holy Friend, you're going to call Him Holy Friend and you're going to know Him in a way, because there are people in this room, many of you first nations peoples that you have a connection into the realm of the Most High, and He's says: I'm going to do something as I call you, as I say to you: You are the upper room and Holy Spirit Himself is going to begin to birth, He's going to begin to hover, begin to birth a new thing, and it starts in Alaska."

TWENTY-FOUR PRAYER

Lord, You prepared Your disciples by grace for the upper room, and we know You are preparing us, calling us to one accord, to seek You. We are dependent upon You to teach us, mentor us, walk with us, talk with us, mold us into that which You desire us to be, for the fire to fall, for the wind to come, for the power of Holy Spirit to descend upon us. Oh Lord, then many will be amazed at the teaching and preaching of Your word, even as Peter preached and thousands came into the kingdom that day. So also, will Alaska be changed.

In *Psalm 135:7 it is says You bring the wind out of Your treasures.* We ask and call for this wind, out of Your treasures Lord. A wind that will change the landscape of Alaska and the people of this land along with this nation.

We know it won't look like anything we can even perceive. But You O Lord, are one who does things suddenly. We want to be ready for You Lord.

We want to know Holy Spirit as our Holy Friend. Show us Your characteristic traits we haven't seen or known yet.

We Long for You Lord. We long for the rivers from the throne room and fruit for the healing of the Nations, that is talked about in *Revelation 22.*

I declare one accord in the people of Alaska. I declare unity is forming and sprouting up all over this Land.

25

A New Highway

August 8, 2019 Chuck Pierce

"There are sounds that will come from Alaska that will set a new course for Kingdom movement.

No longer will you be singing just a song that you have heard others sing, you will be creating sounds that are coming from heaven and from earth, then you will see the Glory move.

This state has always been a part of the apostolic move but now there is a new move.

Once this season has ended and a new move is beginning the love of God is going to burst forth in a new way.

But I say this: You will be known for your sheltering of the movement of the Jews out of Russia.

Get ready, you will be the state that will be called "one new man" has risen in this part of the land.

Get ready, you are moving into a new dimension.

I'm here to announce Gods order has come to Alaska in a new way.

Get ready, get ready, His order has come and you will be known as the place where His presence created a new highway that will affect North America, change the west coast and even enter into Mexico and bring great change."

TWENTY-FIVE PRAYER

Oh, how Glorious, marvelous and mighty You are oh Lord. You alone direct our feet.

We ask You to cover us, protect us and show us how to guard our hearts and minds in this season, in this new Era. We turn our ears to hear the new sound, this new impression that we will hear from heaven and release from this land, setting a new path, new procedures, new movement for Your Kingdom.

We long to release this new sound, this new sound that's from Your throne room.

We long to see the manifestation of Your presence, here in Alaska.

Lord, we thank You for what the past Era brought us.

Lord, don't let us hang on to whatever needs to be left behind, in the past Era. We seek You for a higher level of discernment to know what to pick up and what to release, so we can move forward into the new, this new measurement or dimension that you have ordained. This place we have never been before. We trust You, depend on You, lean on You O Lord, to assist us in getting ready for Your order. That Alaska be known as the place where "one new Man" has created a new highway, a main direct road from this land, affecting this country.

We want to see *Ephesians 2:14* in Alaska. *Our reconciling "peace" is Jesus! He has made Jew and non-Jew one in Christ. By dying as our sacrifice, He has broken down every wall of prejudice that separated us and has now made us equal through our union with Christ.*

We say the walls have been coming down and the union in You, Jesus, is taking place in this land, in a new way. We thank You we are equal in You, nationally, culturally, racially, and gender.

We need Your love Father, Your love touching each of us, spreading across this land with a connecting of hearts, through You. That pure love, that indescribable love, from Your heart Father, it changes us, it changes Alaska, and changes a nation.

For we know it is not by might, or by power, but by Your Spirit.

26

Devotion & Prayer

Prayer by Tim Sheets
August 9, 2019

"Lord, tonight I decree in Jesus name, the outpouring of Holy Spirit, a mega outpouring that anointing to prevail, that will come upon the Ecclesia in Alaska. This entire region, brake forth now.

We pray, release the anointing to prevail upon the northern warriors, release the anointing upon them in Jesus name. Activate the angel armies to arise. And begin to march in alignment with the armies of government of Your kingdom, of Your church Lord on this earth.
We declare Lord, that great boldness is coming upon the warriors now, they are not going to flinch, not backing up, they are arising for such a time as this.

We declare the government of God is coming and making its stand in Alaska. And in this region, we declare the shift of Your kingdom is now coming into this realm like it's never been seen before. We declare that the new Era is now accelerating. So now Lord, we set ourselves in agreement and in alignment with what You said, and we start to declare, accelerate, accelerate, accelerate.

Kingdom of God accelerate. Accelerate. Accelerate Your mind to us, accelerate signs and wonders. Accelerate Your miracles, accelerate the healing.

Lord, accelerate the harvest, the harvest of multiplied thousands and thousands of souls. Lord may that net be full. We declare Lord, that all around Anchorage, this entire region, this entire state, prodigals come home. We declare to those listening in any way, if they are in a cave in any way, if you are in a cave or in a den, come out of your cave, become a part. Let the aggression of the King arise. Let aggression begin to arise up inside of you. Pray that prayer of the apostles.

Lord I pray this. That all the houses of worship that are represented here, grant that great boldness be upon them, to declare Your word, without compromise.

And that signs and wonders and miracles be done in the name of Jesus. Amen".

27

Olam

August 9, 2019 Dutch Sheets

"Eternity is Olam
He has put Olam, that nature, that ability to discern the times, to move with Him through history, at the right time, He has put that in your hearts. Right time discernment is in your hearts.

He has put Olam in Alaska.
He said: This is My entry point to the ancient of days.

The Lord was saying: The giants are coming down".

TWENTY-SEVEN PRAYER
Prayer by Dutch Sheets

So, Lord, we just speak into the church of Alaska, and we say, manifest not only Elohim, Yahweh, not only Jehovah Jireh, Shalom, or El, or Adonai. Manifest OLAM.

The eternal God, who declared victory from the beginning, who knows what will happen in Revelation 22, before He ever wrote the first word in Genesis 1. Who has it all figured out. Who has every age decreed. This is what I do here, this is what I will do here. This is what I will do here and this is what I will do thru Alaska here. This will flow into the nation and the nations and the very harvest will come, because I say right time miracles, right time words, right time harvest for this season, and I have people ready who will reach down in faith and grab situations, individuals who need Olam to come through now and pray over this Land. Let Your greatness manifest in a new way in this hour. Let angels be sent to orchestrate, prepare, bring gifts, messages, and war for us in the heavens at this right time season, so beautiful things can happen.

And we just say now Olam is in our hearts, eternity is already in us. We partner with the God who is the same yesterday, today and forever, who knows the end from the beginning, we are partners of the Ancient of Days.

So, let right time miracles start happening in Alaska, miracles of salvation yes, but miracles of healing, signs and wonders, and incredible proportion that would cause amazing in Your people. That would grab the attention of the entire State, perhaps the entire Nation, do things, that have not been seen before, so that masses will hear and believe.

We call out the Spirit realm into the natural realm this awakening, this revival, this manifestation, this harvest, this fullness. We say let there be a manifestation of the dominion of King Jesus, we call it from the heavens into Alaska right now.

Kingdom come, will of God be done now in Alaska.
We say from here all the way down the west coast even across the great Pacific the manifestation of Olam goes forth from this place. So, we call that into earths realm, we say Isaac come forth, Acts 3 miracles take place. Fullness of time, manifest.
In Jesus Name, Amen.

28

Breakthrough Highway

August 9, 2019 Chuck Pierce

"The Lord says: It's Me causing the fish to go in a new direction. It's Me causing new trails to be uncovered. The paths will be uncovered as new paths, and Alaska will be the place where the ancient paths will be uncovered as new paths, because you have never uncovered fully the ancient paths and made them a new path for today.

We are calling forth this breakthrough highway that is going to come out of Alaska back down through the west coast and it is going to multiply and multiply, and California will either change or it will shake so violently and quiver so violently that those in California, will say "God is in our midst" and you will hear this.

The Lord says: This is just the beginning of what I'm about to do on the west coast and I'm going to pour My Glory all over Alaska and move forward.

Alaska you cannot get dull and forget the level of warfare.
Alaska is the last territory that will be the key to the warfare to all of Americas future.

There will be world powers warring over this. The word, I gave in 1993, I saw an invasion in Alaska. Now Alaska is constantly in the news of the war over this territory. I say now is the time, to start overthrowing, the resisting forces and watch the strongholds crumble, so you can establish the next move of God in Alaska."

TWENTY-EIGHT PRAYER

Lord, we hear You, our ears are turned to hear, our hearts are turned to walk in the obedience of Your design for us. You oh Lord, own the land, the fish, the animals and all that are in the earth, they all belong to You, for the earth is the Lords and all it contains…

We incline our hearts to see and hear.
Your word talks of the mystery of faith in *1 Timothy 3:9*, and the mystery of the Gospel in *Ephesians 6:19*. And we turn our ears to hear and eyes to see the mystery in the history of this land. That there is an uncovering of ancient, old paths that existed for a very longtime. That You will make new paths. Show us Lord. Lead us. We thank You for reserving this mystery for an appointed time.

We do agree and call forth the breakthrough highway Lord, that place of moving through and beyond obstacles, with sudden advancement in areas destined by Your Kingdom plan. This highway that will open up, a way, a route, a thoroughfare from Alaska to the Lower states of America with new paths, new beginnings, not used before.

Father, we ask for Your angelic assistance in moving forward, and keeping us from becoming dull, or slow and sluggish or with lack of intensity for Your purpose. We repent for the times we have slipped into this dulled atmosphere. We say now, "NO more"!
We engage in the battle to Americas future, we will bring down strongholds in Your name Lord, according to Your word. *Luke 10:19 says You have given us the authority to trample on snakes and scorpions and everything that comes up against the power of Your name, against Your Kingdom.* We know You have brought us to this place, our battle is not against flesh and blood.

We claim and decree over Alaska: *Luke 10:19. We have been given Kingdom power over all the power of the enemy.* The enemy is not allowed to retaliate against us.

We carry Your dunamis power and Your exousia authority in this hour into this new era.
May we steward those things You have for us, may we steward them well, to produce good fruit.

29

Mantle of War in Alaska

August 10, 2019 Dutch Sheets

"Part of this season that we have moved into now, this is important for Alaska.

There are certain places, God puts a warring spirit on it.

It's not that they don't have intimacy and other things, but there are just some peoples, some callings, that more than others involve the spirit of a warrior. And we all need to walk in that to a degree, but there are certain individuals, groups of people who are more than others.

Alaska, He has called to be a warring state. There is a mantle on you, Alaska, for that.

One of the significant mantles on this state is war. Warfare, they are a warring people, love humans, lay your life down for people, but in that spirit realm warring nature, that says, I'm here to take out giants.

We say over the state of Alaska, there is a crossing over into the next season. One Era is finished, the next one begins, this is crossing over, Abraham, the one who crosses over.

We say this is a Hebrew company of crossing over people that are moving now into the next phase of destiny on this land.

To be a company of liberators to be a company of warriors, to be an ambassadorial apostolic prophetic company of warriors, for this State and this Nation and even the nations of the earth.

We say decrees will go forth from Alaska that will open the way for the Ancient of Days to come into this State and into this Nation and Nations. We say Alpha and Omega will come into the Nation, Olam Himself will enter through the decrees and prayers of the Alaskan people.

We say to you this day, come into the fullness of who God called you to be and let the DNA of the inheritance that He put inside of you, the very destiny He put in selves of a warring company of people who take out giants."

TWENTY-NINE PRAYER

Father, today we say Yes once again, Yes to your assignment for Alaska for each of us in this land. We say Yes.

Even as you trained and equipped Ephraim and prepared them for war, so also You have trained and equipped us. Yet, Lord , we are so aware of our dependency on You so that we will not turn back in the day of battle. We will be soldiers, armed and equipped for war, in the place where You have us. We will keep covenant, walk in Your ways and remember Your signs and wonders that You have done in this place for Your Kingdom on this land. We say yes, we are engaged and we thank You Father, *Luke 10:19 says, that You have given us authority to trample on snakes and scorpions and all the power of the enemy.*

We step into this new Era, awakened, with eyes looking and ears hearing for the leading of Your Spirit to direct our steps. Even when we make plans, You come in and direct our steps. Thank You, Father.

We need You to show us, walk with us, direct us, as You use this state as one to free others from captivity. We need You to assist us as we walk as agents of the highest rank, authorized to represent You. For we know it is not by might or by power, but by Your Spirit.

For You came to set the captives free. Thank You for Your freedom, so that we can be used to help others be set free. In Jesus Name, Amen.

30

Watch

November 12, 2019 Rebecca Greenwood

"I heard the Lord saying for Alaska: Watch what is going to unfold for you even within the next two years, and the Lord says: You might be known as the untamed frontier, the Lord says: What God is doing in the first nations people even in Alaska is going to begin to rise up from Alaska and it's going to sweep into North America and its going to sweep into Russia.

And the Lord says that you hold the key to unlock even the First Nations People of Alaska and the State of Alaska, that you hold the key in the Spirit what needs to be healed and reconciled between Russia and the United States.

And the Lord says: Watch what will even unfold the next two-three years. The Lord says: I will put Alaska on the map again governmentally and as that is happening governmentally and healing comes on the land that the resources are going to flow in a new way that will bring prosperity, not only to Alaska but even into North America and into Russia.

The Lord says: Watch because you are a hinge State. You are a hinge State like a Nation, that is going to bring healing between Russia and the United States to make history in this time of the Nations."

THIRTY PRAYER

Oh, how we love Your wrap-around presence and Your wrap-around love, Lord.

Without You we are empty and lost, wandering without direction. Thank You for being the Light that directs us and leads us and pours out faith upon us. Let faith arise within this state, even as *Hebrews 11* talks of faith that has gone before us, let faith spark courage within us that we be mighty warriors in battle.

We call forth the unfolding, the unwrapping, the straightening out and expanding of those things that have been closed up and covered within this state.

Lord, show us how to cultivate that which you are doing in the people of this Great Land. Let each of us know our part.

Let the unlocking and the release that You destined to flow from this State, begin. We ask for Holy Spirit guidance and mentorship on how to walk out these next years, so there would be nothing hindering Your plan for Alaska to once again be governmentally on the map. And that healing would continue in and through this land.

Show us how to pray, declare and decree into this land. We call forth those that would steward the resources with righteousness and justice for Your Kingdom purpose. Give us eyes to see further, expand our eyes to see panoramically, deeper, wider, higher. So that when Alaska is a turning point, and the tipping point is upon us, we would walk in Your purpose, making history for Your kingdom. Let us be history makers, let us be Kingdom of God Makers, oh Lord.

31

Fresh Intercession

January 23, 2020 Karen Fink

"I keep hearing over and over, one word, and it's Arise! For the Spirit of the Lord says: The wind of awakening is here! It is a wind that is breaking the slumber and dullness of the past season off of you. I saw bright white lights that surrounded the entire state of Alaska from border to border, not one light was missing, not one light was dull. For the Spirit of the Lord says, Arise shine Alaska, for your light has come and the Glory of the Lord rises upon you. For behold , darkness shall cover the earth and thick darkness the peoples; but the Lord rises upon you and His Glory will be seen upon you.

The Lord says: During this time of awakening, begin to thank Me for My promises, over this State, thank Me for My Glory that is upon the land, thank Me for My Glory that is domed over this State as a golden covering, thank Me for My Glory that will push back darkness, thank Me for My Glory that will release salvation, thank Me for My Glory that you are called to carry this hour, thank Me for My protection upon your State, thank Me for the plans and purposes that I have for this State, Thank Me for the rich destiny that I have for you and this State, and the fragrance of Christ will flow forth from Alaska as a thick anointing to touch the earth and know that from this place of thankfulness, I am now releasing a fresh intercession that will fall upon the people of this land. I am resurrecting a fresh passion for intercession that will sweep you up as I sweep over this land, for you will intercede from My perspective and with My authority. I am resurrecting a fresh desire with a fresh fire to intercede for souls, for prodigals, for the land, for the borders, for the state, for governmental leaders, for the leaders within the church that I am positioning for My Kingdom purposes.

Arise with Me says the Lord, for I am trumpeting a sound over the Great Land to arise and go with Me. Arise and receive this fresh outpouring of intercession that I am releasing in your midst.

Arise and say Yes Lord, sweep me up and I will pray from Your perspective and with Your authority. Arise and say, I will believe and I will receive this fresh mantling of intercession and I will go forth in the power of this new season."

THIRTY-ONE PRAYER

Glory, Glory, Hallelujah, Glory, Glory, Hallelujah, Glory, Glory, Hallelujah, Alaska will march on Lord. We will move forward and Arise.

We thank You for so many promises You have given and spoken over this land called Alaska. We thank you for Your Glory that is upon this land. We thank You that You have a protection over us, as You push back the plans of the enemy, as we press into You. We thank You for a release of salvations, in the harvest that is upon this land. We seek Your wisdom for the harvest Lord. Thank You for the purposes You have always had for Alaska. Thank You that we are here on this land and we get to participate in Your plans and purpose for Alaska. And the beauty of Your attributes that will flow forth from this state.

We press into You for the anointing to steward Your plans well, to steward Your gifts well, and as we are clothed with the mantle of fresh intercession, Lord we press into Your presence, into seeking Your face. May we be bold and courageous in the coming days. May we see from seated with You in the heavenlies, from a vantage point that is for this Era, this time, this season. We long to hear Your heart beat, and feel what Your heart beats for, and see what Your eyes are looking at, and hear what You are saying. We know it is from this place of being low, acknowledging our very breath is from you, that we will move with your heart beat.
Re-fire intercessors Lord, reignite watchmen Lord, set us on fire, with a fire from heaven that man can not put out or man's ways cannot alter.

We will continue to stand in the gap, in intercession, for what You entrust each of us with. In Your presence, we fill up with the oil of Your presence, to arise and move into Your destiny plan for Alaska.

From the Author

M y heart is that this book set many in motion to pray for this great state of Alaska. If you believe the Word of God, and the word says "He directs the steps of the righteous" and you are in Alaska, you must believe He directed your steps here, for such a time as this. That each one here has a part of His plan and dream for Alaska.

The prayers in this book are not intended to be the only prayer for these prophetic words, it is to propel each of us into praying and releasing the sound we each hear, each sound is unique and needed. Collectively we all release a pray, declaration, or decree over this land sending forth a beautiful sound to the Lord. For we all know in part and see in part. Each part is important to shifting this state forward into the future. Into the destiny the Lord intended.

For such a time as this.

"Alaska you have come to an opportunity for fullness.
You have come to a window for a harvest, you have
Moved into a season where you are going to
Experience what you have been hearing.
What the prophets have been saying, and the promises
For breakthrough for signs and wonders.
And miracles, and deliverance.
This is the season for fullness
This is the season of mercy
This is the season of love,
compassion,
And breakthrough."

Dutch Sheets
August 8, 2019

CPSIA information can be obtained
at www.ICGtesting.com
Printed in the USA
JSHW022036200420
5192JS00005B/10